Cornerstones of Freedom

The Powers of Congress

R. Conrad Stein

CHILDRENS PRESS®

CHICAGO

Library of Congress Cataloging-in-Publication Data

Stein, R. Conrad.
    The powers of Congress / by R. Conrad Stein.
        p. cm. – (Cornerstones of freedom)
    Rev. ed. of: The story of the powers of Congress. ©1985.
    Summary: Discusses the role of Congress in governmental
separation of powers, defines the powers and rights held by
Congress, and examines how the balance of power between the
President and Congress has shifted in the last two centuries.
    ISBN 0-516-06696-X
    1. United States. Congress—Powers and duties—Juvenile
literature. [1. United States. Congress—Powers and duties.
2. Separation of powers—United States—Juvenile literature.]
I. Stein, R. Conrad. Story of the powers of Congress.
II. Title. III. Series.
JK1064.S73
328.73'074—dc20   94-36913
                                              CIP
                                               AC

©1995, 1985 by Childrens Press®, Inc.
Revised Edition, 1995.
All rights reserved. Published simultaneously in Canada.
Printed in the United States of America.
1 2 3 4 5 6 7 8 9 10 R 04 03 02 01 00 99 98 97 96 95

On a hot afternoon in August 1974, three worried members of the United States Congress entered President Richard Nixon's office in the White House. They were Senators Hugh Scott and Barry Goldwater and Representative John Rhodes. All three were Republicans, members of the president's own party. The meeting had been called as a result of the shocking Watergate scandal. Evidence pointed to President Nixon's involvement in the cover-up of a 1972 burglary at a Democratic party office in the Watergate building complex. Because the president had apparently committed criminal acts, Congress was now preparing to remove him from office through the process called impeachment.

Senators Hugh Scott (top) and Barry Goldwater (bottom)

President Richard Nixon

With Congress preparing to impeach him in 1974, President Nixon endured dark days in the Oval Office.

After a few minutes of small talk, Senator Goldwater told Nixon that he lacked the votes in the Senate to avoid impeachment. Senator Scott agreed. Rhodes claimed that members of the House of Representatives also favored impeachment.

Nixon thanked the men for coming and told them he would soon decide his next move. Two days later, the president spoke to the nation on television: "Throughout the long and difficult period of Watergate, I have felt it was my duty...to complete the term of office to which you elected me. In the past few days, however, it has become evident to me that I no longer have a strong enough political base in Congress.... Therefore I shall resign the presidency effective at noon tomorrow."

Although Nixon's resignation was expected, his words stunned the nation. Never before had a president resigned from office. The office of the president of the United States is one of the most powerful positions on earth. Yet the Congress, threatening to exercise its own power to impeach, forced him out of office in disgrace. The Nixon resignation is a historic example of the powers of Congress.

Nixon resigns from office.

The powers held by the two houses of Congress were first spelled out in the U.S. Constitution. That document was written at the 1787 Constitutional Convention in Philadelphia. Establishing a Congress was a major task for the convention. A Congress is a lawmaking body composed of individual representatives chosen by voters in their home states. At the convention, an argument developed over how many representatives each state should have in the new Congress. Large states, led by Virginia, wanted the number of representatives to be based on population alone. States with smaller

George Washington speaks at the Constitutional Convention in 1787.

populations, such as New Jersey, wanted all states to have the same number of representatives. A compromise was struck when the delegates agreed to create a Congress with two bodies—the Senate and the House of Representatives. In the Senate, each state would have two representatives, while in the House, a state would have a number of representatives based on its population.

The Constitution

Every state elects two senators to the United States Senate (top). The number of representatives a state has in the House of Representatives (bottom) is determined by the size of the state's population.

The Congress is just one of three branches of the government formed by the Constitution. The branches are: the executive branch (the office of the president), the legislative branch (the Congress), and the judicial branch (the court system headed by the Supreme Court). This system of divided authority is called the separation of powers. The authors of the Constitution clearly intended the largest share of federal power to go to the Congress. Congress was given the right to tax American citizens, the right to spend money, and the right to declare war.

The Constitution also spelled out how a bill becomes a law. Here, too, the convention gave Congress the advantage. After a proposed law is approved by Congress, it is sent to the president for his approval. If the president is displeased with the bill, he may veto it (refuse to approve it). But Congress can override a presidential veto. With a two-thirds vote from both the House and the Senate, the bill becomes a law despite the veto.

When the 1787 Constitutional Convention adjourned, the delegates believed they had created a government with divided authority, but one that would be dominated by Congress. Yet today, it is the president who makes the bold moves, commands the headlines, and generally leads the nation.

*George Washington,
the first president of
the United States*

Why did the president end up with the leadership position that the writers of the Constitution hoped to give to Congress? One reason is that the president, being one person, can make swift decisions on his own. Congress, on the other hand, must vote to resolve a problem. The vote is usually preceded by long debates that can stretch for months and even years.

Early in the nation's history, the president's office demonstrated that it was more efficient than Congress. According to the Constitution, treaties with other nations must be made with the "advice and consent" of the Senate. In 1790, President George Washington went to the Senate hoping to get its opinions on a proposed treaty. Instead of giving Washington the advice he sought, the senators argued among themselves and finally voted to postpone their recommendation. George Washington became furious. According to one senator, "The president of the United States started up in a violent fret [and said], 'This defeats every purpose in my coming here!'" With that, Washington stormed out of the Senate chambers. Since then, no president has asked the Senate for its "advice" before entering into a treaty with a foreign power. Thus, the Congress lost the power to influence the president's decisions in foreign affairs.

President Lyndon Johnson (above, standing at right) sent thousands of American troops to fight in the Vietnam War (right), although Congress was never asked to officially declare war.

The single most important power a government branch can have is the authority to wage war. Here the Constitution gives one direction to the Congress and another to the executive branch. Article One of the Constitution says, "The Congress shall have power to declare war." But a clause in Article Two reads, "The President shall be Commander-in-Chief of the Army and Navy." Today, this is interpreted to mean that the president can order troops, airplanes, and ships to any part of the world to defend the interests of the United States. So a president can wage war without waiting for Congress to make an actual declaration of war.

The Vietnam War was one such "presidential war." From the 1950s to the 1970s, the U.S. military was involved in the conflict in Vietnam —a war that cost thousands of American lives. But at no point was Congress asked to declare war. The executive held the power to continue a war as long as he saw fit. So through the Truman, Eisenhower, Kennedy, Johnson, and Nixon presidencies, U.S. military involvement in Vietnam increased.

Hoping to prevent future presidential wars, the Congress passed the War Powers Act in 1973. This act asserts an important power of Congress—the power of the dollar. The

By staging huge protests in the 1960s and '70s, Americans demanded that Congress end U.S. involvement in Vietnam.

Constitution gives Congress the exclusive right to raise taxes and spend public money. The War Powers Act declares that Congress can refuse to spend money to support a prolonged presidential war. A president must withdraw troops ninety days after they are dispatched unless Congress approves the deployment or grants an extension.

Since the passage of the War Powers Act, the United States has not been involved in a war as lengthy as the Vietnam War. But some presidents have still gone ahead with brief military actions without the consent of Congress. During the Persian Gulf War of 1991, President George Bush never asked Congress to declare war. But a bill was passed in Congress that authorized him to use military force against Iraq. By refusing to ask Congress for a formal declaration of war, recent presidents have affirmed the executive's role as commander-

In 1991, President George Bush steered the American forces through the Persian Gulf War against Iraq.

in-chief. At the same time, they have acknowledged the importance of congressional support for military intervention abroad.

Since the U.S. government's beginnings, the powers of Congress and the president have risen and fallen. During peacetime, the power of Congress tends to increase while the president's authority diminishes. In times of war, the opposite takes place.

The 19th century was the heyday of powerful Congresses. Early in the 1800s, a group of young frontiersmen headed by Henry Clay and John C. Calhoun began to dominate Congress. Because they favored war with Great Britain, they were called the "War Hawks." At that time, Congress was powerful enough to lead the

The congressional "War Hawks" urged the United States into the War of 1812, depicted above.

15

nation into war. The influence of the War Hawks pushed a cautious President James Madison into the War of 1812 with England.

In the decades following that war, the issue of slavery commanded the country's attention. The halls of Congress rang with bitter debates over whether the government should abolish slavery. The arguments were so heated that they sometimes exploded into fistfights. Such

President James Madison

A fistfight breaks out during a congressional debate about slavery.

national figures as Daniel Webster and Sam Houston were members of Congress at the time. With these national figures leading the passionate debate over slavery, Congress captured the attention of the country. The president took a back seat in the headlines.

Congress's years of dominance ended with the first cannon fire over Fort Sumter on April 12, 1861. When the Civil War began, the president took on more influence in national affairs. President Abraham Lincoln held the Union

Fort Sumter is attacked by the South, launching the Civil War.

President Abraham Lincoln (center) meets with his top military commanders during the Civil War.

together during the four-year war between northern and southern states. Lincoln reclaimed presidential powers that previously had been held by Congress. At the start of the fighting, he expanded the army without waiting for congressional approval. He also spent money that never was appropriated by Congress. Meanwhile, Congress looked the other way and allowed Lincoln to lead the country through its darkest period.

After the war ended, Lincoln was killed by an assassin's bullet. With the nation's strongest leader out of the picture, Congress reasserted its powers. In fact, Congress attempted to exercise its ultimate weapon against the president—the power to impeach.

A group called the Radical Republicans held the most influence in Congress in the mid-1860s. In the Senate, they were led by Charles Sumner of Massachusetts and in the House by a feisty Pennsylvanian named Thaddeus Stevens. The Radical Republicans wanted to place the southern states that had rebelled in the Civil War under military rule. President Andrew Johnson disagreed. Johnson had been President Lincoln's vice president, and he intended to carry out Lincoln's lenient policy of restoring the Union through reconstruction. With Congress violently opposed to the president, the stage was set for the nation's most dramatic clash between two branches of the government.

Claiming that President Johnson had violated congressional laws, the Radical Republicans moved to impeach him. The word *impeach* means to accuse, or to charge. To remove the chief executive from office, the House of Representatives must first charge the president with committing a crime. The Senate then must hold a trial to determine whether the president is guilty of that crime. In February 1868, the House of Representatives chose to impeach Andrew Johnson by a vote of 126 to 47. The proceedings then moved to the Senate, where conviction required a two-thirds vote.

The Senate galleries buzzed with spectators as the clash between the president and the

President Andrew Johnson is given a summons to appear at his impeachment hearing in Congress. Johnson was the only president to come so close to being impeached and removed from office.

Congress continued. Emotions boiled and tempers flared. A senator from Maine received a threatening letter saying, "Any Republican senator who is against impeachment need never expect to get home alive." Despite the threats, the Senate vote fell one short of impeachment. Congress could not expel President Johnson from office. If Johnson had been impeached, the presidency likely would have become a weak office that would be forever subordinate to Congress.

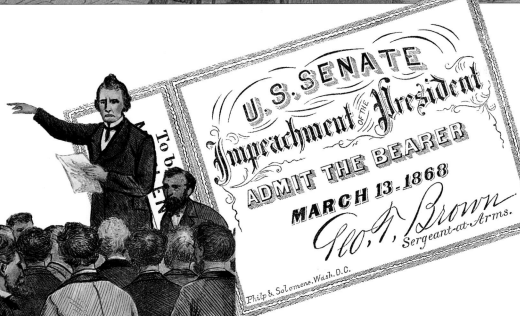

The Senate was gripped by high drama as President Johnson's impeachment was debated (top). Senator Thaddeus Stevens (far left) was a leader of the movement to impeach the president, and is seen here reading his closing argument. So many spectators were expected in the Senate chamber that special tickets were printed (left).

Strong Congresses continued to dominate in the second half of the 1800s. But in the next century, the nation struggled through the Great Depression and two world wars. In those troubled times, distressed Americans looked to the White House for heroic leaders. President Franklin Delano Roosevelt emerged as one of the most popular and powerful presidents in American history. Roosevelt pushed his "New Deal" economic policies through Congress, which helped end the Depression. And when Japan bombed Pearl Harbor in 1941, Roosevelt

President Franklin Delano Roosevelt, who guided the United States through the Great Depression and most of World War II

DEFENSE BUDGET AUTHORITY IN CONSTANT (1988) DOLLARS

brought the United States into World War II. During the war, Congress gave Roosevelt sweeping powers to run the nation's economy as well as its military.

As powerful and popular as the president became in the war years, Congress held firmly to some of its most important powers. Perhaps the best example of Congress's primary power is the annual battle of the budget.

The authority to spend public money is one of the basic powers granted to Congress by the Constitution. Therefore, once a year, the

President Reagan's budget director, James Miller, states his case before the Senate Budget Committee in 1988. The struggle to pass the nation's budget has turned into an annual battle between the president and Congress.

23

president must ask Congress for a budget to run the huge executive department. The president's budget request often conflicts with the wishes of Congress. For instance, in the 1980s, Republican presidents Ronald Reagan and George Bush claimed it was necessary to spend billions of dollars to build up the U.S. military. The Congress, which was often dominated by Democrats, maintained that the public money would be better spent on education or social programs. Every year, the president and Congress locked horns over how to spend the nation's money.

Congress holds many responsibilities besides making laws. It oversees the U.S. Mint, which prints and coins money (opposite page); the U.S. Botanical Gardens in Washington, D.C. (left); and the Library of Congress (below, left), which houses millions of books and famous documents, including the historic Gutenberg Bible (below, right).

John Marshall (above) was the chief justice of the Supreme Court from 1801 to 1835. The nine justices of the Court hear their cases at the Supreme Court Building (top).

The president is Congress's major constitutional rival, but not its only one. The separation of powers system also includes the judicial branch, which is headed by the Supreme Court. The Constitution does not give the Supreme Court the authority to overrule any act of Congress. Yet the Supreme Court has held that power since 1803. A Supreme Court case called *Marbury v. Madison* was settled in 1803. In that case, Chief Justice John Marshall declared that a law passed by Congress is *not* a law if it contradicts

the Constitution. Marshall's landmark decision established a practice called "judicial review." This means that anyone who believes that an act of Congress violates the Constitution can take the case before the Supreme Court. The Court will hear the case and can decide if the law should stand. Judicial review has led to numerous clashes between Congress and the Supreme Court.

The 1993–94 Supreme Court

Studying the powers of Congress is a complicated but fascinating task. For more than two centuries, lawyers, judges, and scholars have debated the rights and restrictions of congressional authority. All the books that have been written on the subject could probably fill a library.

Despite the enormously complex issues surrounding its authority, the Congress will always be the voice of the American people. The Capitol, with its majestic dome that towers over Washington, D.C., is the nation's meeting hall. For years, the stately building has been the site of congressional debates that have made history. It is no wonder that Thomas Jefferson once called Congress "the great commanding theater of this nation."

Inside the Capitol's magnificent dome

GLOSSARY

bill – a proposed law that is brought to Congress for a vote

budget – a plan for raising and spending money

chief justice – the judge who presides over the Supreme Court

compromise – a settlement to a disagreement in which each side gives up some of their demands

Civil War – war between northern (Union) and southern (Confederate) American states (1861–1865)

Civil War

Constitutional Convention – the formal meeting of delegates from all states at which the Constitution was written

delegate – a person authorized to act or speak on behalf of a group

executive branch – the branch of government headed by the president; carries out the laws of the nation

impeach – to accuse or charge with a crime

judicial review – the system in which the courts check the laws of Congress to make sure they are constitutional

judicial branch – the branch of government headed by the Supreme Court; includes all the federal courts of the nation

landmark – holds tremendous importance; *Marbury v. Madison* is considered a "landmark" Supreme Court decision

legislative branch – the Congress; the branch of government that makes laws

House of Representatives

presidential war – a war in which the president orders troops into battle without the consent of Congress; the Vietnam War was a "presidential war"

separation of powers – system in which the three branches of government (executive, judiciary, legislature) have different powers, thus guarding against one branch taking too much control

unconstitutional – a law or act of Congress that a court has decided violates the Constitution

veto – to strike down or disagree; the president can veto an act of Congress by refusing to sign a bill it has passed

TIMELINE

1776	Declaration of Independence signed
1781	Articles of Confederation adopted
1783	Revolutionary War ends

U.S. Constitution signed **1787**
First U.S. Congress meets **1789**
Bill of Rights ratified **1791**

1803 Supreme Court's *Marbury v. Madison* decision

1812 ⎫
1815 ⎬ War of 1812

1861 ⎫
1865 ⎬ American Civil War
1868

Congress attempts
to impeach
President
Andrew Johnson

1914 ⎫
1918 ⎬ World War I

1929 The Great Depression begins

1939
World War II ⎰ **1941** Pearl Harbor attacked by Japan
1945

1950

1973 War Powers Act
1974
1975

Vietnam War
(heaviest American
involvement: early
1960s–1973)

1991 Persian Gulf War

President Nixon
resigns from
office

INDEX *(Boldface page numbers indicate illustrations.)*

PHOTO CREDITS

Cover, ©Cameramann International, Ltd.; 1, Bettmann; 2, Architect of the Capitol; 3 (all three photos), 4, AP/Wide World; 5, UPI/Bettmann Newsphotos; 6, *Washington Addressing the Constitutional Convention,* 1856 by Junius Brutus Stearns. Oil on canvas, 37 1/2 x 54 inches. Virginia Museum of Fine Arts, Richmond. Gift of Edgar William and Bernice Chrysler Garbisch; 7, 8 (bottom), Photri; 8 (top), SuperStock, Inc.; 10, ©White House Historical Association, photograph by The National Geographic Society; 12 (both photos), 13, 14, AP/Wide World; 15, 16 (bottom), Stock Montage, Inc.; 16 (top), Bettmann; 17, Stock Montage, Inc.; 18, AP/Wide World; 20, Stock Montage, Inc.; 21 (top and bottom left), Bettmann; 21 (center), North Wind Picture Archives; 22, 23, AP/Wide World; 24 (left), Photri; 24 (right), 25 (bottom right) ©Cameramann International, Ltd.; 25 (top), Mae Scanlan; 25 (bottom left), 26 (top), Photri; 26 (left), North Wind Picture Archives; 27, ©The National Geographic Society, courtesy The Supreme Court Historical Society; 28, ©Ping Amranand/SuperStock, Inc.; 29, 30 (bottom), Photri; 30 (top), 31 (top left), Stock Montage, Inc.; 31 (bottom left), AP/Wide World; 31 (bottom right), Bettmann

ADDITIONAL PICTURE IDENTIFICATIONS

Cover: *The United States Capitol*
Page 1: *The old House of Representatives*
Page 2: *Henry Clay speaks before the U.S. Senate in 1850.*

STAFF

Project Editor: Mark Friedman
Design & Electronic Composition: TJS Design
Photo Editor: Jan Izzo
Cornerstones of Freedom Logo: David Cunningham

ABOUT THE AUTHOR

R. Conrad Stein was born and grew up in Chicago. After serving in the U.S. Marine Corps, he attended the University of Illlinois, where he earned a B.A. in history. He later studied in Mexico, where he received an advanced degree in fine arts. Mr. Stein lives in Chicago with his wife and their daughter, Janna.